Photographic Prayers

The Holy Island of Lindisfarne explored through images and words.

by Mary and Mark Fleeson

This first edition published by:
Lindisfarne Scriptorium Limited,
Farne House, Marygate,
Holy Island of Lindisfarne,
TD15 2SJ, United Kingdom.
www.lindisfarne-scriptorium.co.uk

ISBN-13: 978 0 9561402 7 2

10 9 8 7 6 5 4 3 2 1

British Library Cataloguing in Publication Data - a catalogue record for this book is available
from the British Library.

Typeset by Lindisfarne Scriptorium Limited.
Book production and preparation by Burning Light Solutions Limited.
Printed and bound in the UK.

Dedicated to Aurian & Calum who teach us daily how to look at the world with new eyes.

As the wind and the rain expose the stones in the spent Autumn field,
May nothing in me be hidden from my God.
As the trees masquerade as warm winter fires in friendly hearths,
May my spirit blaze in the presence of my God.
As the seas quicken and writhe in the cold eastern gales,
May my heart hasten to love my God more.

His Glory will be shown in the skies and His Majesty in the hills,
His compassion will shine in the eyes of the child
and the earth will cry out His Name.
His creation will bow and then rise up and dance,
in the light of His welcoming smile,
And laughter will replace our lonely wail,
as we take our place at His side.

Distant bell tolls for evening prayer,
Clear sound disturbs the cooling day,
Come,
Come,
Come and worship.

Distant Priory stones, still warm to touch,
Seem to whisper with the scurrying clouds,
Worship,
Worship,
Worship Him.

Grant me the faith to believe
That even when the path is hidden,
You will show me Your way
When the time is right.

Repaired, restored,
Patched, pitched,
Weathered, worn,
Textured, torn,
Bleached, battered,
Salty, spattered.

Restorer, raised, perfect, praised,
Wonderful, wholeness, total, timeless,
Breathed, big-time, saviour, sublime.

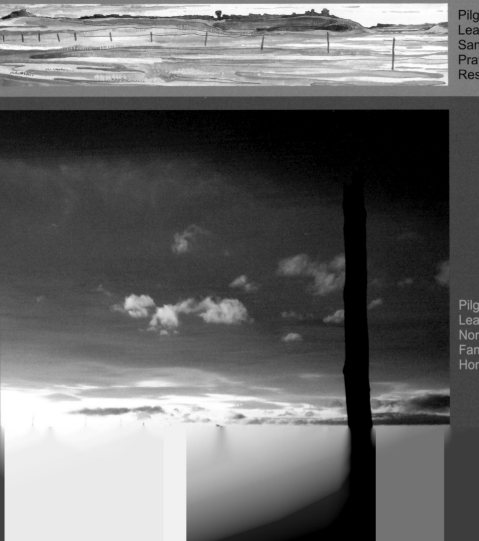

Pilgrim posts calling,
Leading towards
Sanctuary,
Prayer,
Rest.

Pilgrim posts calling,
Leading towards
Normality,
Family,
Home.

As You calmed the waters,
Calm my mind from the undercurrents of doubt.
As You healed the sick,
Heal my spirit and free it to be wholly Yours.
As You restored the dead,
Restore me at my end and my beginning.

High place, God place, reach out and touch His face place.   Holy site, Spirit site, sense His power and might site.
Blessed location, peaceful location, pray for the world and our nation location.

The tide rises through the sand,
Let Your Love grow.

Seeping slowly, filling every ripple and channel,
Let Your Love smooth the scars of conflict.

Distant waves, white edged, advance with inevitable triumph,
Let Your Love defeat every strategy of the enemy.

The sun transforms the water into purest gold,
Let Your Love change our hearts.

Apocalyptic skies,
Swirling, whirling.
Strangely still where I stand.
The sun,
On my right,
Makes the sky look so black.
The snow so white.

I could have missed this sight today.
I may have missed the tension in the air.
I would not have heard the muffled silence.

God, grant me the courage to experience life,
The energy to seek out the new,
And the patience to learn from the past.

You are my refuge and my strength,
You make a high place for me to dwell in safety.
You surround me and protect me,
You turn my enemies into friends
And my friends into family.
You are my refuge and my strength.

Here on the Island, gulls wheeling, circling, crying.
Know His peace,
Surrounding like the tide, washing, cleansing, weeping.
Know His heart,
Love reaching, holding close, understanding, giving all.
Know His pain,
As our outstretched wings fly away.
Know His joy,
When we come home.

Tranquil land, turbulent sky, today I feel the same.
All around me is the chaos of life,
Decisions to be made,
Plans to be fulfilled,
People needing parts of me
Until there's nothing left...

But still there is a quiet, deep within my soul.
Part of me that is protected,
Comforted by His touch,
Encouraged by His word,
Supported by His Spirit
And blessed beyond my dreams.

Sometimes it's hard
to believe in the promises,
And have faith
in words penned so long ago.

Sometimes it's hard
to live out the life,
And be the person
we've been told we can be.

Sometimes it's hard
to see the rainbow,
And not think
'It's just sunlight in rain'.

Sometimes it's hard.

God knows.

Ancient walls, softened and worn,
Sculpted by wind and rain.
Shelter.
Refuge.
Haven.
Ancient paths, follow today,
Locals walk, pilgrims tread.
Discover.
Explore.
Renew.

Loose layers,
Coming apart at the seams.
Tattered tarps,
Fraying at the edges.
Peeling pitch,
The mask is slipping.

Boat cut in half,
Overturned,
Useful again.

A ruined splendour
In the distance,
But the awe remains.

A blood soaked land
Full of memories,
Washed by the tide.

Ancient prayers,
Faithful adorations,
Join those of today.

As we fall apart,
Heal us.
As our lives unravel,
Mend us.
As our defences crumble,
Love us.

As the tide caresses the shore,
May Your presence soothe my soul.
As the water makes dull stones glisten,
May Your Spirit give colour my life.
As the grasses bend in the breeze,
May I be flexible to Your will.
As the sunlight turns water into jewels,
May my life be transformed.

Create in me
a clean heart,
O God,
That I may reflect
Your purity.

Instill in me
a peaceful heart,
O God,
That I may reflect
Your harmony.

Build in me
a strong faith,
O God,
That I may reflect
Your power.

Iron barrel collects the rain,
Reflects with darkened
mirror clarity.
Such is life.
We reflect,
Dimly,
The radiance of God.
But,
On bright days, good days,
Joyful and blessed days,
We sparkle and shimmer,
Like sun on the shore.

Lonely cross,
Remember them, remember Him.
Stone foundations,
Remember the saints who went before.
Peaceful Isle,
Remember the human need to retreat.
Distant hills,
Remember the imperative to return.
Open skies,
Remember to dream without limits.

Summer sun slowly sets,
Slips serenely, silently.
Steals sunshine shadows,
Showing stunning starry sky.

Creator of the Universe,
at the end of this day
May Your peace descend.
May Your love overwhelm us,
May our darkness be fearless,
May our night be restful,
and our day be joyful.

A lonely boat abandoned for a season,
Scarred and stripped by the sand and wind.
Desert by the sea.

A person in a solitary walk through life,
Unaware of the hand that reaches out to hold.
Lonely in a crowd.

A gull flies under windswept clouds,
Its voice like a keening cry, a terrible lament.
Speaks for us all.

A man once hung on a cross alone,
Abandoned, left to carry an unbearable weight.
Left to die. Born to live.

Often the way ahead is hidden,
A turn in the road,
A darkness beyond the headlights,
Often the shadows surround.
And yet to the west there is a gentle light,
And to the east a promise of the dawn.
Often the things that frighten,
The looming silhouettes and eerie sounds,
Are benign in the light of the Son.

Clipart.

All the drawn images are taken from artwork by Mary Fleeson.

From the piece 'John 1'.

From 'As the Touch'.

From 'Journey'

Dear Friend,

As we both take photographs when we're out and about on the Island and share cameras, we are never sure exactly who took which photograph, therefore this book has credited us both! We hope you have enjoyed them as much as we enjoyed capturing these unique moments in time. All of the words were written by Mary in response to the images.

Mary & Mark, Holy Island, 2010.

p19
Pilgrim posts from the Island.

p20
Dramatic winter skies.

p21 & 22
Stormy skies with Lindisfarne Castle in the background.

p23
Refuge box on the Causeway.

p24
Birds flocking over a sodden field opposite Popple Well.

p24
Birds flocking (detail).

p25
Birds flocking.

p26
Swallows chatting on the telephone wires over our garden (*I'll name that tune in...*), and a stunning daytime moon.

p 27
Lindisfarne Castle with rain clouds behind.

p28
View towards Sandham with sheep.

p29
Lindisfarne Castle

p30
Walls near St. Mary's Church.

p31
St. Mary's Church.

p32
Peeling upturned herring boat.

And what I think was a buoy of some kind.

p33
Old boat near The Ouse.

p34
Seashore near the Castle.

and grasses on Cuthbert's beach (opposite Cuthbert's Isle, also known as 'Hobthrush' or 'Cuddies').

p35
View from Castle road towards the Village.

p36
This image is a few years old but was taken at the fishermen's huts at The Ouse.

and sunlight on the sea looking from the Castle road, also p48.

p37
Cuthbert's Isle (Cuddies) from the beach opposite.

p38, 39 & 40
Sunsets looking towards the mainland.

p40
Old abandoned boat on The Ouse - it is no longer there but was a dramatic sight for several years.

p41
Panorama of St. Mary's and the Priory taken from the Heugh.

p42 & 43
Sunsets looking towards the mainland.

p45
Late night summer lane between Holburn and Kyloe, on our way home (taken with an iPhone from a moving car!).

About Holy Island

Holy Island is a small Island off the coast of Northumbria, roughly half-way between Newcastle and Edinburgh in the United Kingdom.
The Holy Island of Lindisfarne was key to the Christian faith being spread throughout the North of England in the 7th century A.D. and was the location of a Celtic and then later Benedictine monastic community.

About Mary & Mark Fleeson

We have lived on Holy Island since 1997 and have two children.

Photography has been a passion for both of us since school days and we are delighted to be able to share some of our favourite images of the Island.

For more information about Mary's work, Lindisfarne Scriptorium and our other publications, please visit:
www.lindisfarne-scriptorium.co.uk